BIBLE HEROES
COLORING BOOK

Illustrated by
Page O'Rourke

The purchase of this coloring book grants you the rights to photocopy the contents for classroom use.
Notice: It is unlawful to copy these pages for resale purposes. Copy permission is for private use only.

305800215454

Noah (Genesis 6:9–22)

God told Noah to build a big boat called an ark.
Noah obeyed. Two of each animal got on the ark.
God kept them safe from the flood.

Joseph (Genesis 37:12–36, 43—45)

Joseph's brothers were mean to him. Later, Joseph became an important man. He forgave his brothers and took care of them.

Moses (Exodus 13:17—14:31)

Pharaoh's army was after Moses and his people.
God told Moses to raise his staff over the Red Sea. The water
parted, and the people walked across on dry ground.

Rahab (Joshua 2)

Rahab hid God's men who came to spy on the city of Jericho.
When the city was destroyed, her family was kept safe.

Joshua (Joshua 6:1–21)

Joshua believed God and obeyed Him. Joshua's army marched around the wall of Jericho. Then the walls fell down!

Deborah (Judges 4:4–23)

Deborah listened to God and told people what He said.
The army leader listened to Deborah,
and God's army won the battle.

David (1 Samuel 17)

David loved God. He was a young boy, but God gave him strength. He beat the giant, Goliath!

Elijah (1 Kings 18:16–40)

Elijah prayed for God to send fire to prove to the people that
He was God. God's fire burned up the meat on the altar.
It burned up the wood, rocks, and water, too!

Esther (Esther 3—7:10)

A bad man wanted to kill all the Jewish people.
Queen Esther was a Jew. She risked her life by asking the king
to save her people, and he did.

Josiah (2 Kings 22—23:3)

Josiah was only 8 when he became king. A part of the Bible that no one had read was found in the temple. Josiah read it to the people. They all promised to obey God.

Daniel (Daniel 6:1–24)

The king said everyone had to pray to him.
Daniel prayed only to God. He was thrown into the lions' den,
but God kept him safe.

Stephen (Acts 6:8—7)

Stephen was a preacher. His preaching made some people angry. He gave up his life to tell people about Jesus.

Jesus (Matthew 27—28)

Jesus healed people. He loved them. But some people didn't love Jesus. They hung Him on a cross. He died to save us from our sins. Then God raised Jesus to life again!

Peter (Acts 2)

Peter once lied and said he didn't know Jesus.
He was so ashamed! He asked for forgiveness. Later, he started
preaching, and 3,000 people believed in Jesus in one day!

Paul (2 Corinthians 11:16–32)

Paul was beaten with rods and hit with stones.
He was in 3 shipwrecks. He was put in jail, too.
Nothing would stop Paul from telling people about Jesus!